KANSAS characters

A poster/coloring book

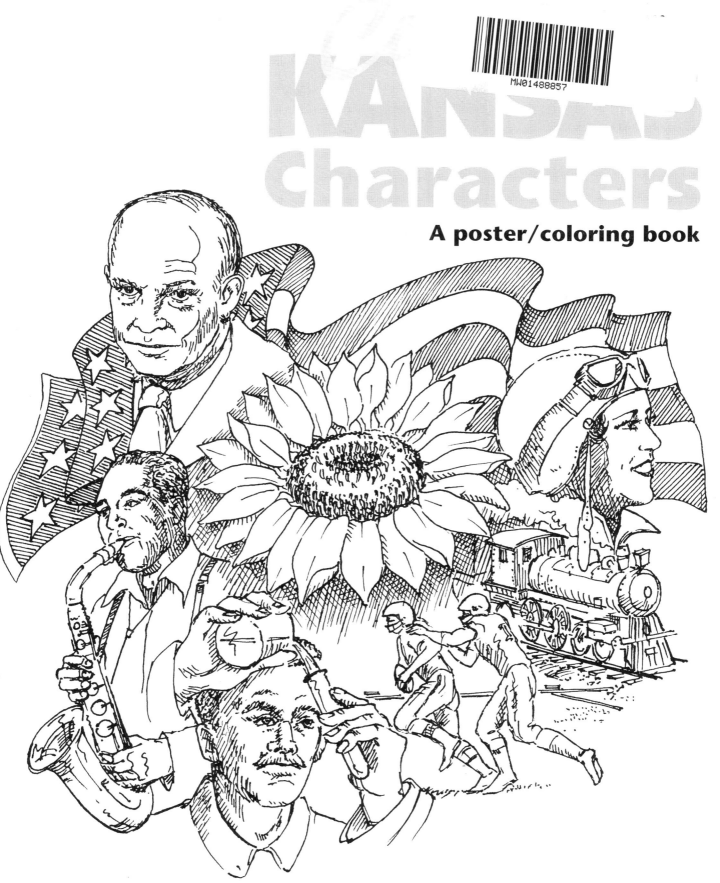

**Kansas Heritage Center
Dodge City, Kansas**

**Artwork by
Phillip R. Buntin**

COLOR KANSAS CHARACTERS
A poster/coloring book

© **1996 Kansas Heritage Center, P.O. Box 1207, Dodge City, Kansas 67801-1207.**

ISBN 1-882404-09-2   An individual purchaser may reproduce materials in this poster/coloring book for personal or classroom use only. The purchase of this book does not entitle reproduction of any part for an entire school, district, or system. Such use is strictly prohibited. Text adapted from the revised edition of 399 Kansas Characters by Dave Webb, © 1994, published by the Kansas Heritage Center.

KIRSTIE ALLEY

Actress

(Born 1951) Kirstie Alley is an actress. She grew up in Wichita and graduated from Southeast High School. After attending Kansas University and Kansas State University, Kirstie worked as an interior decorator in Wichita. Then she moved to California to go into acting. Kirstie's big break came in 1981 when she appeared in a Star Trek movie. Six years later she joined the cast of the popular NBC television comedy Cheers. Ms. Alley still appears in movies and television shows. She also works to protect animals and help people with drug addictions.

3

ED ASNER

Actor

(Born 1929) Ed Asner is an actor who has won several Emmy and Golden Globe awards. He grew up in Kansas City and graduated from Wyandotte High School. Ed began acting after he served in the military during the Korean War. He appeared on stage in Chicago and New York.

In 1961 he moved to California to work on television. Mr. Asner has starred in many movies and television shows. In the 1970s and 1980s fans knew him as "Lou Grant" in two CBS series, The Mary Tyler Moore Show and Lou Grant. He has since appeared in other television shows.

WALTER & OLIVE ANN BEECH

Airplane manufacturers

(1891–1950) (1903–1993) The Beeches built an important aircraft manufacturing company in Wichita. Walter was born in Tennessee. Later he lived in Arkansas City. Olive Ann was born in Waverly. She then lived in Paola and Augusta. In 1932 Walter and Olive Ann started manufacturing aircraft. Their company, Beechcraft, sold thousands of military planes during World War II. After her husband died, Mrs. Beech ran their business. It became part of Raytheon Company in 1980. Beechcraft made all kinds of aircraft, including parts for NASA's space shuttles.

'MOTHER' MARY ANN BICKERDYKE

Nurse and veterans' supporter

(1817–1901) Mary Ann Bickerdyke worked hard to help others during and after the Civil War. She was born in Ohio. During the war she lived in Illinois and worked as a nurse. When she delivered supplies to an Army hospital, she decided to stay and help. For four years Mary Ann traveled with military units, nursing the injured, and gathering food and supplies. After the war "Mother" Bickerdyke moved to Kansas. In Russell and then Bunker Hill she continued her work. She helped ex-soldiers start farming and got aid for them when their crops failed.

6

BLACK DOG

Indian leader

(About 1780–1848) Black Dog was a Native American leader. He was an Osage, born in what later became Missouri. When his father died, sixteen-year-old Black Dog became chief of a band of Osages. His band lived in what is now eastern Kansas. For a time, their village was along the Neosho River, in present Labette or Cherokee County. Chief Black Dog helped his people build one of Kansas' earliest roads. Using stone axes and hoes, the Osages cleared a trail west to hunting grounds along the Ninnescah River. Today it is marked as the Osage Trail or Black Dog Trail.

JOHN 'DOC' BRINKLEY

"Quack" doctor and politician

(1885–1942) John Brinkley was a "quack," a person who pretends to be a doctor. He was perhaps born in North Carolina. In Kansas, John worked in Hays, Axtell, Fulton, and then Milford. The dishonest doctor liked money-making schemes. His most famous was transplanting goat glands into men to make them feel better. The operation didn't help, but thousands had it done. In the 1920s "Doc" sold worthless medicines over his own powerful radio station. Even though his schemes were discovered, Kansans nearly elected him governor in the 1930s. He died in Texas.

GWENDOLYN BROOKS

Poet

(Born 1917) Gwendolyn Brooks is an honored poet. She was born in Topeka and grew up in Chicago. Gwendolyn began writing poetry as a child. She had her first work published when she was thirteen. In 1950 Miss Brooks became the first African American woman to win a Pulitzer Prize, one of the highest awards given to writers. The state of Illinois made her its official state poet in the 1960s. In the 1980s Miss Brooks was chosen to be a poetry consultant to the Library of Congress. To encourage young poets and authors, she sponsors writing contests.

9

JOHN BROWN

Crusader

(1800–1859) John Brown tried to end slavery— by using violence. He was born in Connecticut and grew up in several states. Before the Civil War, he helped slaves escape on the Underground Railroad. In 1855 he came to Kansas and lived near Osawatomie. Citizens argued about allowing slaves in Kansas when it became a state. Brown helped turn the arguments into "Bleeding Kansas." He led a band that raided and killed people who supported slavery. After he and his men tried to steal U.S. Army weapons in Virginia, the radical crusader was hanged.

10

ARTHUR CAPPER

Governor, U.S. senator, newspaper publisher and philanthropist

(1865–1951) Arthur Capper was governor of Kansas from 1915 to 1919. He then served in the U.S. Senate until 1949. There he organized the "farm bloc," a group of senators and representatives from farming states. Arthur also owned several newspapers. He often used his wealth to help Kansas children. Before there were 4-H clubs, he set up youth organizations and loaned members money to purchase livestock. In 1920 he established the Capper Foundation for handicapped children. It still operates in Topeka. Mr. Capper grew up in Garnett and also lived in Longton.

GEORGE WASHINGTON CARVER

Scientist and educator

(1864?–1943) George Washington Carver helped farmers by inventing ways to make hundreds of useful products from peanuts, soybeans, and other plants. As a teenager, George left his Missouri home to go to school in Kansas—at Fort Scott, Olathe, Paola, and Minneapolis. When a Kansas college would not admit him because he was black, he homesteaded near Beeler. He left the state a few years later and graduated from Iowa State University in 1894. Dr. Carver did his research on plants at Tuskegee Institute in Alabama. He taught there for almost 50 years.

12

CLYDE CESSNA

Airplane manufacturer

(1879–1954) Clyde Cessna turned his love of machinery into an airplane manufacturing company. He was born in Iowa but grew up on his family's farm near Rago. As a boy, Clyde enjoyed repairing farm equipment. Later he worked for an implement dealer in Harper. In 1911 he built his own plane. Although he crashlanded a dozen times, he soon learned to fly. Five years later Mr. Cessna built the first plane made in Wichita. By 1927 he had his own manufacturing company there. Today Cessna Aircraft is one of the world's largest makers of small aircraft.

WALTER CHRYSLER

Automobile manufacturer

(1875–1940) Walter Chrysler's name appears on thousands of automobiles. He was born in Wamego and then lived in Ellis. Walter was a talented mechanic. He first worked for railroads in Kansas and other states. Then he became fascinated with automobiles. He bought one—but instead of driving it, he tore it apart and put it back together again and again. By 1916 he was president of Buick Motor Company. In the 1920s he bought his own car company. Today Chrysler Corporation is a major automobile manufacturer. Mr. Chrysler's home in Ellis is now a museum.

WILLIAM F. 'BUFFALO BILL' CODY

Scout, buffalo hunter and entertainer

(1846–1917) William F. Cody helped create the legend of the Old West. He was born in Iowa. As a boy in Leavenworth, Bill hauled hay for the Pony Express. Later he fought in the Civil War and worked as a scout for the U.S. Army. He became "Buffalo Bill" when he hunted buffaloes to feed crews building the Union Pacific Railroad across western Kansas. In the 1880s Cody put together "Buffalo Bill's Wild West." This action-packed show presented the Old West—in fact and fiction—to eager audiences in the United States and Europe. Mr. Cody died in Colorado.

15

DON COLDSMITH

Author and doctor

(Born 1926) Don Coldsmith writes books that are enjoyed by millions of readers. He was born in Iola. His father was a minister and Don grew up in several towns: Parsons, Independence, Coffeyville, and Fort Scott. After World War II he became a doctor in Emporia. Don began writing in the 1960s when he started a newspaper column about horses. In 1980 he wrote the story of a lost Spanish soldier who brought horses to Indians on the Great Plains. That book turned into a popular series, the "Spanish Bit Saga." Millions of Dr. Coldsmith's books have been sold.

DON'T SPIT ON SIDE WALK.

SAMUEL CRUMBINE

Doctor and public health crusader

(1862–1954) Samuel Crumbine was Kansas' first full-time state public health officer. He warned people, "Don't spit on the sidewalk," and "Swat the fly." In 1909 he helped Kansas become the first state to outlaw "common cups" at public wells and water fountains. Dr. Crumbine also helped pass laws to stop water pollution and the sale of impure food and medicines. He was born in Pennsylvania and came to Kansas in the 1880s. Before he worked in Topeka, Samuel practiced medicine in Spearville and Dodge City. He moved to New York in the 1920s.

GLENN CUNNINGHAM

Runner

(1909–1988) Glenn Cunningham was an Olympic runner. He was born in Atlanta. His family moved to Rolla when he was five. Two years later, Glenn's legs were terribly burned in an accident. Doctors said he would never walk again. But Glenn fought pain and infection— and proved them wrong. To exercise, he ran. He ran so well he set world records at Elkhart High School and then Kansas University. He also competed in the 1932 and 1936 Olympics. Later he lived in Emporia, Cedar Point, and Augusta. Mr. Cunningham ran homes for needy children.

CHARLES CURTIS

Representative, senator and vice president

(1860–1939) Charles Curtis was the first Native American to be vice president of the United States. He was born near Topeka. Because one of his grandmothers was part Kansa, or Kaw, he was a member of that tribe. Charles spent part of his boyhood on the Kansa reservation near Council Grove. He also lived in Topeka. As a teenager he rode racehorses and was called "Indian Boy." Later he became a politician. For over 30 years he spoke for Kansas in the U.S. House of Representatives and Senate. In 1928 Mr. Curtis was elected vice president under Herbert Hoover.

JAMES DICK

Pianist

(Born 1940) James Dick has given concerts across the United States and Europe. He has even performed in New York City's famous Carnegie Hall. James grew up on a farm near Hutchinson. He took his first piano lessons at the age of five. By the time he graduated from high school, he had won several state music contests. In college James studied piano at the University of Texas and the Royal Academy of Music in London. He now lives in Texas. Each summer Mr. Dick sponsors music festivals for young musicians from around the world.

BOB DOLE

Representative and senator

(Born 1923) Bob Dole is a politician. He became one of Kansas' two U.S. senators in 1968. He was born and grew up in Russell. He attended the University of Kansas at Lawrence and then served in the U.S. Army during World War II. Later, he graduated from Washburn University at Topeka. Bob was first elected to office in 1950 as a state representative. He was later county attorney from Russell County and a U.S. representative. In the Senate, he was an important and powerful leader. In 1996 Senator Dole resigned from the Senate to run for president.

DASHING KANSAN!
Prof. L. L. DYCHE,
At the Melvern Opera House, Feb. 8,
AFTERNOON AND NIGHT.

Dyche is now the most popular Arctic Ex-
plorer and that she has se-
ury 8.

Greenland he carries you

NORTH POLE,

es, taken from Nature.

LEWIS LINDSAY DYCHE

Naturalist and educator

(1857–1915) Lewis Lindsay Dyche was a naturalist and educator. He taught at the University of Kansas and often went on scientific expeditions in the summer. In 1910 he became the state fish and game warden of Kansas. He helped write laws to protect endangered species. Lewis came to Kansas as a boy. He and his family lived in Osage County and near Auburn. After he graduated from school in Emporia, he attended KU. Mr. Dyche's work is displayed at the University of Kansas' Dyche Museum of Natural History, which he helped design and fill with exhibits.

CUTTER SEARCHING HERE FOR FLIERS

SAN FRANCISCO

Midway Is.

2410 Miles

SHANGHAI

HONG KONG

Wake I.

HONOLULU

HAWAIIAN IS.

MANILA

PHILIPPINE IS.

Guam

1800

P A C I F I C

Kingman Reef

O C E A N

NEW GUINEA

Lae

3700

Howland I.

EQUATOR

PORT DARWIN

Samoa Is.

Pago Pago

Fiji Is.

SUVA

AUSTRALIA

BRISBANE

SYDNEY

AUCKLAND

NEW ZEALAND

AMELIA EARHART

Aviator

(1897–1937?) Amelia Earhart was a famous aviator. She was born at her grandparents' home in Atchison. Because her father traveled in his work, Amelia spent much of her childhood in Atchison. As a woman pilot, Miss Earhart set many records. In 1932 she became the first woman to fly alone across the Atlantic Ocean. Three years later she was the first pilot to fly from Hawaii to the U.S. mainland. In 1937 she tried to fly around the world. But over the Pacific Ocean, Amelia, her navigator, and their plane disappeared. Her Atchison birthplace is now a museum.

WYATT EARP

Law officer and gambler

(1848–1929) Wyatt Earp became famous as a law officer in the Old West. He was born in Illinois and lived in several states before he came to Kansas. Wyatt was hired as a policeman in Wichita in 1875. The next year he moved to Dodge City. There he worked as a law officer and gambler. He left Kansas in 1879. Later he lived in Arizona. In the small town of Tombstone, Wyatt and two of his brothers had a gunfight with outlaws at the OK Corral. After he died in California, a long list of books, movies, and television shows have made Mr. Earp a legend of the Old West.

DWIGHT D. EISENHOWER

Army general and president

(1890–1969) Dwight Eisenhower was born in Texas but grew up in Kansas. He served in the U.S. Army for over 30 years and became a top general. During World War II he commanded the Allied forces that freed Europe. "Ike," as he was called, was elected America's 34th president in 1952. After he left office in 1961, Dwight and his wife Mamie lived on a farm near Gettysburg, Pennsylvania. His Kansas hometown, Abilene, is the site of the Eisenhower Center. It includes Mr. Eisenhower's boyhood home, presidential library, museum, and burial chapel.

25

FREDERICK FUNSTON

Army general

(1865–1917) Frederick Funston was an honored soldier. He was born in Ohio and grew up near Iola. Fred attended the University of Kansas. Before he joined the U.S. Army, he had adventuresome jobs in the western United States, Central America, and Cuba. In the Spanish-American War he received the Congressional Medal of Honor and became a general. In 1906, he was in charge of clean-up after the terrible San Francisco earthquake. Some felt if he had not died in 1917 he would have led America's forces in World War I. General Funston's Iola home is now a museum.

DOROTHY GALE

Fictional farmgirl

(Created 1900) Dorothy Gale is an imaginary Kansan known to millions of people. She was created by L. Frank Baum, a writer. Dorothy was the main character in his best-selling book The Wonderful Wizard of Oz. She also appears in other books by Mr. Baum—and the popular movie The Wizard of Oz. Although Dorothy and her dog Toto meet interesting friends in the land of Oz, she wants to return home to Aunt Em and Uncle Henry on their Kansas farm. Today you can visit Dorothy's House in Liberal. In Sedan, you can walk down the Yellow Brick Road.

BILL GRAVES

Governor

(Born 1953) Bill Graves was elected Kansas' forty-third governor in 1994. He was born and grew up in Salina. Bill graduated from Kansas Wesleyan University in Salina in 1976. He then attended the University of Kansas. In 1985 he was appointed assistant secretary of state. A year later he was elected secretary of state. His first lieutenant governor was Sheila Frahm. She was the first woman elected to that office in Kansas. Governor Graves appointed Mrs. Frahm to the U.S. Senate in 1996. Gary Sherrer of Wichita then became Kansas' lieutenant governor.

EMANUEL & MARCET HALDEMAN-JULIUS

Authors and publishers

(1889–1951) (1887–1941) Emanuel and Marcet Haldeman-Julius made it easy for readers to own books. Emanuel Julius was born in Pennsylvania. He moved to Kansas in 1915 to work for a newspaper in Girard. His wife, Marcet Haldeman, was born in Girard. (They combined their last names after they were married.) To help make books available to many people, Mr. and Mrs. Haldeman-Julius published small paperbacks that sold for just a few cents each. Their "Little Blue Books" series included thousands of different titles, and books they wrote themselves.

FRED HARVEY

Restaurant chain operator

(1835–1901) Fred Harvey enjoyed pleasing hungry customers. He was born in London and came to America as a teenager. Later he lived in Leavenworth. There Fred was unhappy with the poor food and service train passengers received at railroad restaurants. In 1876 he opened a restaurant for a Kansas line, the Atchison, Topeka & Santa Fe. Mr. Harvey's good food, clean surroundings, and polite service made his Topeka restaurant very popular. Soon he ran "Harvey Houses" all along the Santa Fe Railway. His efficient waitresses, or "Harvey Girls," were part of his success.

STEVE HAWLEY

Astronaut

(Born 1952) Steve Hawley has flown in space. He was born in Ottawa and graduated from high school in Salina. Steve earned a degree from the University of Kansas. He became an astronaut in the late 1970s. In a 1990 flight of the Discovery, he placed the Hubble Space Telescope in orbit.

Before he retired from space flight, Dr. Hawley spent 412 hours in space—including three space shuttle missions. He then became a NASA administrator in Houston. Exhibits at the Kansas Cosmosphere and Space Center in Hutchinson tell about Steve Hawley and other Kansas astronauts.

31

STAN HERD

Artist

(Born 1950) Stan Herd creates jumbo-sized art. He grew up in Protection where he drove a tractor on his father's farm. Later Stan moved to Dodge City. There he first painted historical murals on buildings. In 1981 he used his talent and tractor-driving skills to turn a Kansas field into a portrait of Satanta, a Kiowa Indian leader. Stan has since completed more "crop art." Some of his designs are plowed into the soil. Others use crops that change textures and colors as they grow. Mr. Herd's work has been seen on television and in magazines. He lives in Lawrence.

Home on the Range

Oh, give me a home where the buf-fa-lo roam,

an-te-lope play;...

BREWSTER HIGLEY

Doctor and poet

(1823–1911) Brewster Higley wrote the words to the state song of Kansas. He was born in Ohio and came to Kansas in 1871. Two years later he wrote a poem, "My Western Home." In it the doctor shared his feelings about living on the prairie near Gaylord. His young neighbor, Daniel Kelley, set the poem to music. "Home on the Range," as people called it, was soon popular. In 1947 it became the Kansas state song. Although others later published their own arrangements of "Home on the Range," Kansas historians believe it was written by Dr. Higley and Daniel Kelley.

LANGSTON HUGHES

Poet and author

(1902–1967) Through his writing, Langston Hughes told of his dreams for racial freedom. He was born in Missouri but spent most of his boyhood in Lawrence. He also lived in Topeka for a time. As a child, Langston faced racial prejudice. As an adult, he included his experiences with prejudice and discrimination in his writing. But his poetry, novels, short stories, plays, and other writing also included his hopes for racial equality. Mr. Hughes lived in several states and foreign countries. He spent many years in the Harlem section of New York City.

WAR CORRESPONDENT

PEGGY HULL

Newspaper journalist

(1889–1967) Peggy Hull was the first American woman to be an official war reporter. Her name was Henrietta Goodnough when she was born near Bennington. Then she lived in Marysville, Oketo, and Junction City. There she first worked for a newspaper. Later, at a Minnesota paper, she began using the pen name Peggy Hull. In 1918 she became the first American woman to report from a war zone. Peggy's stories helped readers in the United States understand World War I. Miss Hull continued her combat reporting through World War II. She died in California.

THE HOME OF MENTHOLATUM

THE GREAT JAPANESE SALVE
MENTHOLATUM
AN EXTERNAL APPLICATION FOR CURE OF ALL INFLAMMATIONS
SORE THROAT HEADACHE EARACHE PILES CATARRH RHEUMATISM
BRUISES COLD SORES CHAPPED HANDS CROUP
HAY FEVER INSECT BITES &C
APPLY TO PART AFFECTED

YUCCA CO

ALEXANDER HYDE

Medicine manufacturer

(1848–1935) Alexander Hyde developed a medicine used by millions. He was born in Massachusetts and came to Kansas as a teenager. After working in a Leavenworth bank, Alexander moved to Wichita. There he went into business selling soap, cough syrup, and other products. In 1894 he introduced a medicine he helped develop. "Mentholatum," as it was called, was soon very popular. By 1906 it was the only product he sold. For many years Mr. Hyde made Mentholatum at his Wichita factory. After his death the company moved to New York.

MY
SPIRITUALS

by
Eva A. Jessye
Illustrated by
Millar of the
ROLAND COMPANY
Edited by
Gordon Whyte & Hugo Frey

ROBBINS ~ ENGEL, Inc.   New York

EVA JESSYE

Singer, choral director, actress, composer, poet, and author

(1895–1992) Eva Jessye was very talented. She was born in Coffeyville, and also lived in Caney and Iola. After she attended college, Eva taught music. In the 1920s she moved to New York City where she got several jobs as a singer. Soon she organized musical groups for radio programs and commercials. Eventually she directed choirs for movies and Broadway musicals. She also appeared in several films, and wrote poems and music. In 1979 Miss Jessye returned to Kansas for a time. She was an "artist-in-residence" at Pittsburg State University. She died in Michigan.

37

MARTIN & OSA JOHNSON

Explorers, photographers and authors

(1884–1937) (1894–1953) Martin and Osa Johnson became world-famous explorers and photographers. In the 1920s and 1930s they made movies, gave lectures, and wrote books about animals and native cultures in Africa, Asia, and the South Pacific Islands. Martin was born in Illinois. He grew up in Kansas, at Lincoln and Independence. Osa was born and raised in Chanute. After Mr. Johnson was killed in an airline crash, Mrs. Johnson continued their work. The Martin and Osa Johnson Safari Museum in Chanute tells the story of these famous Kansans.

NANCY KASSEBAUM

Senator

(Born 1932) Nancy Kassebaum's father, Alf Landon, was governor of Kansas and a candidate for president when she was a small child in Topeka. Years later, Nancy served on the Maize school board. In 1978 she was elected to the U.S. Senate. This made her the first female senator from Kansas—and one of the few women ever elected to the Senate. Her work there was praised by voters and fellow politicians. In 1995 Senator Kassebaum became the first woman ever to chair a major Senate committee. At the end of her third term she retired to her farm near Council Grove.

EMMETT KELLY

Circus clown

(1898–1979) Emmett Kelly has been called one of the greatest clowns of all time. He was born in Sedan and moved to Missouri as a boy. After he worked as a cartoonist, Emmett joined a circus as a trapeze artist and clown. To look different than other clowns, he dressed in tattered clothes and painted his face with a big, sad frown. His character, "Weary Willie," worked in the Ringling Brothers and Barnum & Bailey Circus. He also appeared on television and in movies. Mr. Kelly often ended his act with Willie trying to sweep away light from a spotlight shining on the stage.

ALF LANDON

Governor

(1887–1987) Alf Landon was a popular politician for many years. He was born in Pennsylvania and moved to Kansas when his father took a job in Independence. Alf graduated from the University of Kansas. He became successful in the oil business and also worked in politics. Soon he was chairman of the Kansas Republican party. He was elected governor in 1932. In 1936, during his second term, Republicans nominated him for president. Although he was defeated by Franklin D. Roosevelt, Mr. Landon continued to be a respected political leader. He died in Topeka.

JIM LEHRER

Television journalist

(Born 1934) Jim Lehrer is a respected broadcast journalist. He lived in Wichita and Independence as a boy. After his father's Kansas bus company went bankrupt, Jim and his family moved to Texas. There his teachers encouraged him to use his writing skills. After college, he worked as a reporter and editor at Dallas newspapers. Then he took a job with a public TV station. In 1975, he became an anchorperson on the McNeil-Lehrer NewsHour, now called the The NewsHour with Jim Lehrer. The award-winning news program is broadcast on PBS stations around the country.

WILLIAM B. 'BAT' MASTERSON

Law officer, gambler, and newspaper journalist

(1853–1921) William B. Masterson lived through exciting times in the Old West. "Bat" was born in Canada. He and his family moved to Kansas in 1871. His parents settled near Sedgwick but Bat soon headed west to hunt buffaloes. In early 1876 he and his friend Wyatt Earp became policemen in Dodge City. The next year he was elected sheriff there. Until 1879 he was busy with horse thieves, train robbers, murderers, and Indian raiders. Later he was a gambler in several western states. When he died, Mr. Masterson was a sports reporter for a New York City newspaper.

ADA McCOLL

Pioneer

(1870–1956) Ada McColl was a pioneer in early-day Kansas. She was born in Iowa and moved near Medicine Lodge as a small girl. Her family left Kansas in 1884, but returned two years later and settled near Lakin. In 1893 Ada's mother photographed her with a wheelbarrow full of "cow chips." (Like other settlers, the McColls burned the dried manure as fuel.) Miss McColl later moved back to Iowa, but over the years her Kansas photograph has been published many times. Now the "Cow Chip Lady" on the prairie is one of the state's most-recognized pioneers.

HATTIE McDANIEL

Actress

(1895–1952) Hattie McDaniel was the first African American to win an Oscar. She was born in Wichita and moved to Colorado when she was a child. Hattie performed with traveling theater companies until the 1930s. She then moved to California and sang with groups on the radio and in movies. In 1939 she got an acting part in the well-known film, Gone with the Wind. When she received an Oscar for her performance, Miss McDaniel became the first African American to win that important award. In all, she appeared in over 300 movies.

CHARLES, KARL & WILL MENNINGER

Mental health pioneers

(1862–1953) (1893–1990) (1899–1966)

Charles Menninger and his sons Karl and Will founded an important hospital in Topeka. Charles came to Kansas in the 1880s. He and his wife lived in Holton for a time. Then they moved to Topeka. There he established the Men-ninger Clinic. When his sons Karl and Will joined the staff, the three Dr. Menningers worked together to develop new treatments for mental illnesses. Today other family members work at their Topeka facility. Menningers', as it is now known, is respected around the world.

JAMES NAISMITH

Educator, minister, and doctor

(1861–1939) James Naismith is called the "father of basketball." He was born in Canada and came to America after he graduated from college. While teaching at a Massachusetts YMCA in 1891, James invented a new game. In it, teams tried to score points by tossing a ball at a target.

When he used two peach baskets as targets, his game had a name—basketball. Later James became a minister and a doctor. In 1899 he moved to the University of Kansas. He was the campus minister and first KU basketball coach. Dr. Naismith remained in Lawrence until he died.

CARRY NATION

Crusader

(1846–1911) Carry Nation crusaded to stop people from drinking alcohol. She was born in Kentucky and came to Kansas in 1890. Saloons were illegal in the state at that time, but drugstores sold liquor as "medicine." To help stop the practice, Carry angrily marched into Kansas drugstores. With a hatchet, she smashed furniture, and barrels of beer and whiskey. Across America and Europe she preached against drinking alcohol. At the same time, she raised money for alcoholics and their families. Mrs. Nation's home in Medicine Lodge is now a museum.

CHARLIE 'BIRD' PARKER

Jazz saxophonist and composer

(1920–1955) Charlie Parker loved jazz from the first time he heard it in his hometown, Kansas City. At 17 he began traveling with jazz bands. He earned the nickname "Bird" when he asked someone to roast a chicken that had been run over in the road. Charlie formed his own jazz bands in the 1940s. With trumpeter Dizzy Gillespie he developed a new form of jazz called "bebop." Unfortunately, he also abused drugs— and died at age 34 in New York City. Music experts have called Mr. Parker one of the most important jazz musicians and composers.

49

GORDON PARKS

Photographer, author, poet, composer, and filmmaker

(Born 1912) Gordon Parks' talent is recognized around the world. He was born in Fort Scott. When he was a teenager, he left Kansas to live in Minnesota with his sister. In the 1930s he joined a traveling orchestra. Later he began taking photographs. His skill with a camera got him a job with the U.S. government. Eventually he was a photographer for Life magazine and other important publications. He has also written several books, composed music, and produced and directed movies. His book and film, The Learning Tree, tells the story of his boyhood in Kansas.

50

SAM RAMEY

Opera singer

(Born 1942) Sam Ramey has sung in operas around the world. He was born in Colby, and also lived in Winona and Quinter. He took voice lessons in school, but opera wasn't for him—one of his favorite singers was Elvis Presley. Sam then attended Kansas State University and Wichita State University. While at WSU he began singing opera. By 1973 he was the leading bass soloist for the New York City Opera. Since then he has sung in operas and on television around the world. Mr. Ramey has made more albums than any other American-born bass singer.

BARRY SANDERS

Football player

(Born 1968) Barry Sanders has set records as a football player. He grew up in Wichita and attended Wichita North High School. At Oklahoma State University he was recognized for his talent on the football field. During his junior year at OSU he won the Heisman Trophy, the highest honor for a college football player. He became a running back for the the Detroit Lions in 1989. The next year he was the NFL's leading rusher. In 1991 Mr. Sanders was named Pro Football Player of the Year. His success with the Lions has earned him several million dollars a year.

BIRGER SANDZÉN

Artist and educator

(1871–1954) Birger Sandzén was one of Kansas' best-known artists. He was born in Sweden. As a young man, Birger came to Lindsborg. There, at Bethany College, he taught art for over 50 years. He created over 3,500 paintings, drawings, woodcuts, and other works of art. They are full of color and power. Mr. Sandzén especially enjoyed painting wildflowers and outdoor scenes from Kansas and other western states. He gave many paintings to schools and libraries around Kansas. The Birger Sandzén Memorial Gallery at Bethany College is named in his honor.

SATANTA

Indian leader

(1830?–1878) Satanta, or White Bear, was a chief of the Kiowa tribe. He grew up on the Great Plains and became well known in Kansas during the 1860s. At peace meetings he was called the "Orator of the Plains." But sometimes his talk about peace was just talk. In one case,

the Kiowa leader accepted a peace gift of a U.S. Army officer's uniform—and then wore it when he stole horses from Fort Dodge! When Satanta took part in more raids, the Army held him hostage in hopes his people would surrender. He died in a Texas prison.

'SOCKLESS' JERRY SIMPSON

Representative

(1842–1905) Jerry Simpson was a colorful politician. He was born in Canada and moved to the United States as a child. After working as a sailor on the Great Lakes, Jerry moved to Kansas. He farmed near Holton and then ranched near Medicine Lodge. When times got tough for ranchers and farmers in the 1890s, he joined the Populist, or "people's" party. He earned the nickname "Sockless" when he claimed he was too poor to buy socks. For three terms, Congressman Simpson worked hard in Washington to represent Kansas people. He later lived in Wichita.

Ho for Kansas

rethren, Friends, & Fellow Citi
I feel thankful to inform you th
REAL ESTAT
AND
Homestead   Associ
Will Leave Here the
15th of April 18

In pursuit of Homes in the Southw
Lands of America, at Transportat
Rates, cheaper than ever
was known before.
For full information inquire of
Benj. Singleton, better known as old Pap,
NO. 5 NORTH FRONT STREET.
Beware of Speculators and Adventurers, as it is a dangerous thing
to fall in their hands.
Nashville, Tenn., March 18, 1878.

BENJAMIN 'PAP' SINGLETON

Crusader

(1809–1892) Benjamin Singleton helped former slaves find new lives in Kansas. He was born in Tennessee—as a slave. At age 37 he escaped from slavery and moved to Michigan. There he helped other escaped slaves. After the Civil War, Benjamin returned to the South. He told ex-slaves about the advantages of moving to Kansas. He then led several hundred people to "Singleton's Colony" in Cherokee County. "Pap" also raised money to help new settlers. Mr. Singleton's work paved the way for thousands of "Exodusters"— ex-slaves who moved to Kansas in the 1870s.

CHARLES STERNBERG

Paleontologist

(1850–1943) Charles Sternberg and his sons made important fossil discoveries. He was born in New York and came to Kansas as a teenager. His interest in fossils eventually led to a career in paleontology. Charles and his sons George, Charles, and Levi went on fossil-hunting expedi-tions and sold their discoveries to museums around the world. In Kansas Mr. Sternberg lived in Ellsworth and Lawrence. Today, the Sternberg Museum at Hays displays fossils the Sternberg family discovered. The museum was started by George Sternberg.

MILBURN STONE

Actor

(1904–1980) Milburn Stone was a popular movie and television star. He was born near Burrton, and grew up there and in Larned. After he graduated from high school, Milburn joined a traveling theater company that gave shows across Kansas and Oklahoma. Then he worked on stage in several cities across the country. In 1936 he got a part in a movie, the first of over 150 films he made. Mr. Stone is best-known as "Doc Adams," a fictional Dodge City doctor in the TV series Gunsmoke. The popular Western ran on CBS for 20 years and is still seen in reruns.

58

CLYDE TOMBAUGH

Astronomer

(Born 1906) Clyde Tombaugh is an astronomer who made an important discovery. He was born in Illinois and came to Kansas when he was a teenager. Clyde's family lived on a farm near Burdett. There he spent many nights peering through a telescope he and his father had built.

As a young man, he went to work at the Lowell Observatory in Arizona. In 1930, while studying photographs he had taken through the observatory's large telescope, Mr. Tombaugh discovered a new space object. It was a planet in our solar system that no one had ever seen before—Pluto.

EMPORIA GAZETTE

VOL. 7.   EMPORIA, KANSAS, THURSDAY, AU

WILLIAM ALLEN WHITE

Newspaper journalist and author

(1868–1944) William Allen White was one of Kansas' best-known citizens. He was born in Emporia and grew up in El Dorado. After Bill graduated from the University of Kansas, he worked at newspapers in El Dorado and Kansas City. Then he bought his own paper, the Emporia Gazette. In 1896 an editorial he wrote was reprinted around the country. Soon readers everywhere enjoyed his newspaper articles and books. Mr. White's friends included several presidents and many famous authors. The "Sage of Emporia" was respected around the world.

LAURA INGALLS WILDER

Author

(1867–1957) Laura Ingalls Wilder wrote popular children's books. She was born in Wisconsin. When Laura was a little girl, her family moved to Kansas. They built a cozy log cabin in Montgomery County. There they enjoyed a frontier Christmas, escaped a frightful prairie fire, and saw tall Indians dressed in skunk skins. The Ingalls family then left Kansas and lived in several other states. Many years later, in Missouri, Laura wrote about her childhood. Mrs. Wilder's Little House books have since been enjoyed by millions. Little House on the Prairie tells of her life in Kansas.

JEANNE WILLIAMS

Author

(Born 1930) Jeanne Williams is an award-winning author. She was born near Elkhart and spent part of her childhood in Stafford. Then she lived with her grandparents in Missouri. Jeanne decided to be an author when she was in the fifth grade. In 1957 her first book was published.

Since that time she has written over 60 books that have sold over 10 million copies. Some of her novels are about children, and others feature women. Mrs. Williams enjoys including history in her books. Although she now lives in Arizona, Kansas is one of her favorite story settings.

LYNETTE WOODARD

Basketball player

(Born 1959) Lynette Woodard is a world-class basketball player. She was born in Wichita and thrilled crowds as she played on Wichita North High School's girls basketball team. At the University of Kansas Lynette led her Jayhawk team to three straight championships. She also set sev-eral records, including a college-career total of 3,649 points. In 1984 she was captain of the U.S. women's team that won an Olympic gold medal. Miss Woodard then became the first woman to play for the world-famous Harlem Globetrotters. She later played basketball in Italy and Japan.

LORRAINE 'LIZZIE' WOOSTER

Educator and state superintendent of public instruction

(1868–1953) Lorraine Wooster was the first woman elected to a state office in Kansas. She moved to the state from Ohio as a teenager. After graduating from high school in Beloit, she taught there and in Salina. Later she wrote and published textbooks. In 1918 she was elected superintendent of public instruction in Kansas. As the state's "head teacher," she was strict. "Lizzie" told school instructors they couldn't dance, smoke, or wear makeup or short skirts. When she ran for reelection, she lost. Miss Wooster left Topeka in the 1930s and moved to Illinois.

783